Wilted Flowers of Beauty

Alejandra White

BookLeaf Publishing

Presentation by *BookLeaf Publishing*

Web: www.bookleafpub.com

E-mail: info@bookleafpub.com

ISBN: 9789357441537

First edition 2023

This book is dedicated to my faith, passed loved ones, the mom who gave me up, and the one who took me in. It's also dedicated to my sisters. I love you all more than you know.

ACKNOWLEDGEMENT

Every set back is only a set up for something greater.

PREFACE

The poems in this book may seem all over the place and there are some trigger warning to be aware of. These triggers include; anxiety, depression,abuse,and ptsd. These poems are my story of struggle, growth, and most importantly faith.

Moving On OR Looking Back?

2023, it's supposed to be a new year, new me
right?
so why is it the same past demons I'm having to
fight
I can't get out of my head
my anxiety keeps screaming
wondering what pain is coming next
I want to let go, but my traumas have a bond that
they hold
I'm so worried about becoming my mom
Repeating her patterns
Re-creating her toxicity of relationships
I look in the mirror
The true me is who I miss
All I see is broken pieces of my heart Shattered
like glass
So afraid to take a chance in fear of getting hurt
or hurting someone who doesn't deserve it
The part of me that is her
The part I hide so well
Not even the ones closest to me can tell that
inside I'm screaming
My hurt wants to be let out
My walls want to be let down

Every time I take a step back
Abandonment and grief are waiting to greet me
all over again
My heart is like a wilted flower
Begging for water and love
so it can grow
It keeps being put inside a box
Carried around like a toy for their convenience
Brokenness isn't just a chapter in my book It's
sewn into the spine of the story
All the writers of my love had the same plot
And my heart is waiting on an author with a
special pen
One who takes time to truly think about the
words he's writing on these fragile and rare
pages
But it's scared to have a beautiful story
In fear that it is fiction
And will end like all the rest
My eyes beg for someone to see how brightly
they shine
Even through the pain hidden within the
changing colors
My smile cries out for some one to adore It's
specialness
My vitiligo wonders if someone will ever be
attracted to
The glow as it grows

Surrounding and covering every inch of my
temple
My body art is curious
If anyone will be an awe
of the decor they have created
My mind overthinks
If anyone is patient enough
To calm my anxiety
As my mouth overflows with words,
questions, and most of all apologies
The words,"I'm sorry", like to pour out
And spill into almost every conversation
In fear that
I've done something wrong
Maybe if I sit quiet
And be the gift
That just keeps on giving and pleasing
Then they won't walk away
But they always do
My niceness is a weapon
Used against me
My power
I'm taking back
But it's new
2023, new year, new me
Maybe, just maybe, this will be the year
My traumas are set free

Screaming In Silence

Fears, they're screaming at me,
insecurities are taunting me,
and hope is neglecting me while doubt is taking
ownership consuming me

My breathe is slowly being stolen by anxiety
Smiles are painted on trying to compensate for
the pain resting in my eyes
Prayers, they want to come out but the words are
being shy as they hide intertwined with tears that
flow like rivers down the face of an overly nice
doormat known as me
but answers to the names baby, Alli, bestie,
daughter, sister, etc.
an endless flow of nicknames that are only a
cover up for the benefits package I'm used for

Everyone is so quick to place me in a box
but no one reads or notices the warning label
saying, "Fragile,handle with care"
It's always overlooked by the positivity
packaging
Decorated in care,love, and a heart so big it's a
buffet of forgiveness,mercy,and grace
All of this wrapped up in glitter

Until they decide I'm too much then what?

My price tags goes on clearance as my
loneliness discounts the hurt
Marking down my value only to please my users
and abusers
"Please stay. Don't go. Fight for me. I'm worth
it,I promise." Through the aching bones and
cracking in my voice my inner child cries out
What did I do wrong? Why did they leave? How
can I be better?
All of these questions pound on the door
belonging to my soul
as it beckons for someone to hear and rescue the
brokenness living in the tower of my shame

"Get up child,take my hand. I'll protect you"
says the whispers of faith
The only companion to never walk away
The name of my grace
My protector has been looking after me
Putting me on the strongest soldiers list year
after year
When I don't remember submitting a resume
It must be a mistake right?
Having a job I'm not qualified for
Wrong
No mistake was made. The king called my name

"My child, you are royalty" he speaks over me.
"I heard those silent screams, trust in me. You
are stronger than you think and a braver warrior
than you have been led to believe"

Overlooked Hurt

You broke my heart
I restored it
You broke it again
Why did I go back
Maybe my love for you was in vain
I didn't fall completely
Your eyes spoke the silent truth of the potential
resting in your soul
Beauty as if they were oceans
My gaze fell into them so deeply
In awe of amazement
A sugar coated bee
Bumbling excitement
Underneath your words hid
Lies, deception,and disloyalty
Thought you were my person
Like Luke and Padmé
The force your presence had was undeniable
I'll be there for you always
even just as a friend
I used to hold out hope
Maybe if I fought hard enough
I would be enough
It doesn't work that way
When the one you thought wanted you

Was only deceiving you
But it's okay no more I'm sorries are due
You're debt is paid
I've dealt with the pain
Healed through me and my faith
I'm happy now on my own
Our journey is done
I'm walking away out of love
Love for myself and my sanity
Maybe one day your mirror wrapped in vanity
will break
Our memories I'll cherish
The chapters in our story are protected
I'm sorry for the chances you neglected

Shadows of Protection

Verse after verse I've read the words
Odds have been placed against me
The calling I have is one they can't see
Scripture guided me
With the grain of a mustard seed
I stand firm in faith
The plan of my life
It is written
No other explanation needs to be explored
It won't make sense
The things that should've took me out
Built me up
A stronger soldier I became
Overflowed and drenched in darkness
Not knowing it was the shadow of his wings
Gracious is he that has protected me

I Choose You

I choose you
When it's easy
When it's hard
Through the good
And through the storms
I still choose you

When I'm hurting
When I'm upset
When I'm mad or angry
When I'm tired and want to be alone
I still choose you

In times when you feel like breaking
I'll do my best to hold you together
When you try to push me away and shut down
I'll stand beside you and stick around
When you're struggling and don't know what to
do
I'll fight with you and help figure things out

Through the beauty and
Through the pain
I still choose you
All your flaws

I'll embrace
All your insecurities
I'll show you their beauty
All your doubts
I'll help you work them out
Every problem I'll look for a solution
Every tear I'll wipe away
If you need to scream and yell
I'll listen
If you just need a hug or cuddle
I'll give it
Because I still choose you

I choose you through it all
The good and the bad
Your flaws and insecurities
Your doubts and fears
I choose it all
I choose you not because it's easy
But because you're worth it

You see the love I have for you isn't
a love you only when you make me happy type
love
It's a love you even when I can't look at you
type love
It's not a love you only when it benefits me type
love
It's a love you no matter what type love

My love for you isn't a conditional or limited
type love
It's an unconditional and limitless
type love

We can argue
We can fight
Get on each other's nerves
We can laugh
We can cry
We can make memories
Whatever is it that we may do
At the end of the day
I still choose you

Dear Mama

I know it's been a while since we last talked
But at least I can't say
That I haven't tried
Maybe if you had answered it would've worked
Maybe if it wasn't for our language barrier we
could've spoke
Maybe you just weren't home
Maybe, maybe, maybe just maybe
You see there are so many questions I have
But for every one
I have an excuse already created
In your defense against myself
These intrusive thoughts
Have my mind captivated
You play the blame game
Blaming everyone but yourself
How is it possible
How are you not exhausted
Having to keep up with all of your lies
Throughout the course of all these years
You destroyed me
You apologized
You traumatized me
You apologized
You do all these things

Then you apologize
As if your apology is some kind of an eraser for
all the marks and scars you have engraved into
my brain
But the thing is
Those intrusive thoughts
Are written down in ink
Burned in my brain
Unable to be erased
You picked me apart
As if every piece you took
Somehow completed you
You must have mistaken
My life for a revolving door
Every time you come back
You leave all over again
The same process happens
 As if you are stuck on a loop
The same broken record
Keeps spinning and yet
After all this time
I am still afraid
To remove the needle
In fear of never knowing
If it'll be the last time
I hear you at all
It might be the same song
But it's the only lyrics you know
 We play this game

Of forgive and forgive
Except its only me playing both parts
Part one
You tell me something
I want to hear and take it away
So I play defense
Part two
I tell you I forgive you anyway
And just like that you disappear
All over again
You would think
After all this time
That I have grown up
And became an adult
I wouldn't fall
For your childish ways
Yet here we are
I keep on the same path
Hoping for a different ending
I guess our story isn't one
I'm not ready to stop writing
Even though every chapter
Ends the same way

Hardest Goodbye

I know I've said goodbye
Many many times
But you were the hardest one of my life

False Hope

I thought what didn't kill you
Is supposed to make you stronger
But it's not
It still hurts
All this time has past
But the pain still last
I can't keep doing this anymore
The pain is too great
The hurt is too deep
My breath feels like it's fading
Motivation is draining
I feel like I'm drowning
Drowning in memories
Only making it harder
To keep going
Still forcing myself
To stay strong for everyone else
I guess I forgot
How to be strong for myself
You were my anchor
The one who kept me going
But now it's weighing me down
I can't get up
But I don't want to anymore
I've tried to overlook the hurt

It keeps coming back
Flooding in at moments least expected
Making it difficult to keep going
To keep making it through
Smiling feels like a chore now
Forcing myself to try and be happy
Because I know I deserve to be
But how I can I be
I need you by my side
I miss our moments
Everything about you shined
Liked nothing ever before
Missing you everyday
I can't take this heartache
I'm trying to keep pushing forward
But feels like I'm falling backwards
Watching my world crumble
You held it up
You held my heart
Now it's broken
You're the only one who cherished it
Reminding me of my purpose
Now I'm fighting battles internally
Day by day I want to give in
But your voice remains inside of me
Telling me it's going to be alright
Doesn't feel like it right now
If you're looking down watching over me
I could really use one of your hugs

Take me back to the way it used to be
When it was just you and me

One Last Chance

If I had one last chance
I would hold you tight
and tell you
everything is alright
I miss you here
But I know you're safe
I wanna know everything
What's it like
The streets of Gold
If I could just hold you
One last time
I might never let go
Like the good old days
We could laugh all day
I wanna hear all about everything
You can tell me your stories
The ones I've heard a thousand times
I miss the way
Your face would light up every room
If I had one last chance
I'd make it right
Anything left unsaid
We were close and I need you to know
I need you now more than ever
It's just not the same

Going everyday
Without hearing you say
All those things you used to say
If I had one last chance
To hear I love you and say it back
To see your smile
It's been a while
I miss you here
Next to me
And everything
But I know you're safe so it's okay
I'll see you again someday

When I fall

When I fall down on my knees
I feel a peace like never before
You show me something Lord
When I can't see
You're always there when I'm in need
Or down in agony
Through my dreams
Through worship songs
I praise your name all day long
Verse after verse I learn something new
How great thou art
And the story starts
In a lions den and through the storm
You brought them through and made them new
My sins you wiped away
You gave me grace
Break every chain
In the power of your name
You give me confidence
And this is how
I fight my battles
With just a little talk
I'll fly away
Cause I saw the light in your name
My God fights for me

And saves the day
I trust the word of my Lord
If Jesus said it
I believe it
And did I mention
I can only imagine
Cause on that old rugged cross
Everything changed
In the power of his name I rejoice
Cause I can't even walk without holding his
hand
By the power of his blood I am set free
No weapon formed against me shall prosper
The alpha and omega
In Jeremiah
He said he has a plan for me
In Timothy
He said be strong in grace
His love is my embrace
On this foundation I will raise
My voice and shout
The glory of his name

Wonder Warrior

When disaster struck
She slayed her own demons

My Blessing

Unexpectedly you came in like
A knight in shining armor
My eyes flooded with tears
Of overwhelming joy
It feels surreal
Bringing me closer to my faith
A love I have only read about
Not sure what I did to deserve it
But I'm beyond blessed
To have met you
It's still so new
But better than anything I've known
Everything that makes me unique and different
You labeled a gift from God
Making me feel beautiful in a whole new light
Feeling like royalty for the very first time

My No Told Him Yes

I didn't want to let him in
He kept asking until my no turned into a fine I
guess
I wish that night would leave my head
Asked him if we could wait
He said okay
As he continued what he wanted
As if somehow my no meant yes
Over and over this apparent useless word kept
spilling out of my mouth like a broken record
My head continued to spin
Pushing him off me again and again
I can't, I'm in pain, this hurts
Those were my words until finally the night
came to an end
The bruises might have healed
But the pain I'll never forget

Wilted Love

Instead you chose to place flowers upon the
grave of my hope and trust in you

Am I Deserving

I don't really know how to explain it
Everything seems so complicated
I want you here
But I'm scared to let you near
Can I let you in
Can I trust again

Maybe I'm just too damaged
Maybe that'll never change
Am I just a phase
Am I just in my head

Is there meaning in the things you've said
I don't have doubts in you
I have doubts in me

Heart of Gold

A heart so big
A piece of it has been given
To every person it's comes across
All expect the one
Staring back in her reflection
All it sees then
Is broken pieces
Waiting to be put back together
Too afraid to ask for help
I'm fine
I can do this
I'll figure it out
Her eyes flowing with silent waterfalls
Baggy clothes hide the insecurities
That feel exposed in the discomfort of her
self-consciousness
Dressed head to toe
In other people's opinions
A heart that wants to be protected
But feels selfish
For not loaning it to someone else
She gives and she gives
But saves none for herself
No time to get emotional
In case someone else needs her help

Night after night she spends alone
Worrying about those
Who have no intention of sticking around
Those who don't have space
For her in their heads
Are the ones who take up the most in hers
She can't help it
Too nice is written on her name tag
Too forgiving is her description
A heart of gold
Overthinking tells her she deserves
Nothing other then a lump of coal
Wishing sometimes
That's what her heart was made of
Don't make them
Even the slightest bit upset
They might leave
Strength is in her eyes
But fear has taken over her soul

Maybe Next Time

The balloon of air
In my lungs is deflating
A boulder
Slowly pressing against my chest
Shame, guilt, and fear
Accompany my shoulders
Nightmares take over my sleep
Waking me up every couple hours
Panic starts to set in
Unsure why
I want to cry at times
Fighting back the tears
Can't let anyone see
I'm drowning
But refuse to ask for help
I'm fine I always am
Burdened down and everything
Maybe next time
I'll truly be okay

Identity Crisis

Every time I came close
To figuring out who I was
A new piece of identity was revealed
That was hidden from me
In perfect timing
For me to have no idea who I am
All over again

Missing Me

Sometimes I miss the old me
The optimism I once had
My smile that disappeared
My joy that faded
My hope
My faith
I miss everything
Who I used to be
Pure before my tragedy
I miss feeling whole
I miss who I was before
Before heartbreak
Before understanding
Before I knew what
I would have to go through
Before I allowed toxic people in
Before I knew anything
Other then happiness
I miss the old me
Lost myself
Somewhere along the way
I'm afraid
The old me is too far away

Depression Hides Behind The Smile

Facing my demons all around
Faking a smile for the crowd
Can't keep pretending I'm okay
I said I'm fine
What if I told you it was a lie
In reality I can't sleep at night

I'm Called

A new calling has approached
Prayer is where I go
I'm not qualified
But I'm called
They don't see it for my life
But I'm called
Filled with self-doubt
But I'm called
Odds are against me
But I'm called
They counted me out
God counted me in
Like David, Moses, and Daniel
This "nobody" has been chosen
Time to fight in new battles
He hand picked this soldier
Building me up
As the world knocks me down
I stand firm in faith
And fix my crown

9 789357 441537